T

BLACK BOOK OF

SMOOTHIES

• *Smoothies for Any Time, Reason or Season* •

RUTH CULLEN

ILLUSTRATED BY KERREN BARBAS

PETER PAUPER PRESS, INC.
WHITE PLAINS, NEW YORK

FOR MY EVER-THIRSTY
FAMILY AND FRIENDS, AND FOR JAY,
THE SMOOTHEST GUY AROUND

Designed by Heather Zschock

Illustrations copyright © 2003 Kerren Barbas

Copyright © 2003
Pete Pauper Press, Inc.
202 Mamaroneck Avenue
White Plains, NY 10601
All rights reserved
ISBN 0-88088-470-3
Printed in Hong Kong
7 6 5 4 3 2

Visit us at www.peterpauper.com

THE LITTLE BLACK BOOK OF

SMOOTHIES

CONTENTS

INTRODUCTION 6

BEFORE YOU START 8

• Tips for Scrumptious Smoothies . . . 9

• Fruit and Veggie Facts 14

• Other Important Ingredients 41

SMOOTHIES FOR ANY TIME . . 45

Breakfast Blends 46

Liquid Lunches 55

Afternoon Delights 64

Evening Elixirs 72

SMOOTHIES BY THE SEASON . 83

Spring Sippers 84

Summer Shakes 93

Fall Frosties 102

Winter Freezes 111

SMOOTHIES FOR
ANY REASON 121

Energy Boosters 122

Health Helpers 131

Sanity Savers 140

Special Occasion Smoothies 149

INDEX OF SMOOTHIES BY
PRIMARY INGREDIENT 158

INTRODUCTION

S o you want to eat healthier but find that your busy life leads you to the drive-through window more than you'd care to admit? Well, dunk those donuts in the trash and forget the burger and fries—it's time to discover the world of Smoothies.

Bursting with flavor and loaded with nutrients, Smoothies are the perfect way to grab a quick, nourishing meal on the go. Armed with a blender, fresh fruit, and a little creativity, you will astound yourself with delicious, satisfying blends that hit the spot just about any time of day.

The Little Black Book of Smoothies is chockfull of Smoothie recipes for any time, season, or reason—yours to follow or modify using ingredients that suit your individual tastes and/or dietary needs. And herein lies the beauty of Smoothies: they're your creations—your choices, your blends, your delights.

You'll never think about fast food the same way again.

Happy blending!
R. C.

before you start...

TIPS FOR SCRUMPTIOUS SMOOTHIES

FRUIT AND VEGGIE FACTS

OTHER IMPORTANT INGREDIENTS

TIPS FOR SCRUMPTIOUS SMOOTHIES

ALWAYS USE FRESH, SEASONAL PRODUCE. The most flavorful Smoothies contain fresh, seasonal fruits and vegetables. Use your senses to assess the quality of the produce you buy. As a general rule, fruit should be sweet-smelling and free from any visible blemishes or bruises. Most fruits should be firm to the touch but should give a little when pressed, with the exception of apples, which should be firm. Whenever possible, use organic fruits and vegetables to avoid removing vitamin and fiber-rich skin that otherwise might contain pesticides and wax. Of course, you should always wash fruits and vegetables in warm water before eating. When buying canned or frozen fruit, look for fruit packed in water or juice, and not in heavy, sweetened syrups.

STOCK YOUR FREEZER WITH FRUIT! Find frozen, unsweetened fruit in your grocer's freezer, or prepare fresh fruit for freezing as follows: wash and dry fruit; peel and remove seeds (if necessary); cut into small chunks; place in sealed plastic freezer bags or containers; and freeze. Most fruit freezes in about 30 minutes and will last for a few weeks, although flavor wanes over time. While most fruits stand up well in the freezer, some, namely pineapples and citrus fruits, do not. For added frostiness in your Smoothies, simply pour fruit juices into ice cube trays and crush cubes before blending. If you dry berries thoroughly before freezing, they won't form a solid mass when they freeze.

BUY A GOOD BLENDER! These days, you can walk into just about any discount retailer and buy an excellent blender for about the same price as a tank of gas (car, not SUV!). You can't go wrong with most models, especially those featuring high-speed motors, powerful, ice-crushing blades, and multiple speed settings. Many cooks prefer glass containers over plastic, as plastic tends to get scratched.

CRUSH ICE BEFORE BLENDING. If you're not fortunate enough to have an ice-crush-

ing feature on your freezer, and you forgot to purchase a big bag of crushed ice, then you'll need a few pointers on getting the job done the old fashioned way. Place ice cubes inside a seal-able plastic bag, leaving a little air in the bag before closing. Wrap bag in dish towel, place on solid surface, like butcher block or gran-ite, and pound with kitchen mallet until suf-ficiently crushed.

ADD INGREDIENTS TO THE BLENDER IN THE RIGHT ORDER. Strange but true, the order in which you add Smoothie ingredi-ents to your blender can either speed or slow the process. It can also minimize the dulling effects frozen ingredients can have on your blender's blade. To avoid the need to start and stop your blender repeatedly when its contents do not combine properly, I recommend adding ingredients in the following order: first, juice or liquid; next, soft solids, like yogurt or fresh fruit; and last, frozen fruit, frozen yogurt, or ice.

BLEND SAFELY! Never remove the lid from your blender while it's blending and don't place fingers, utensils, or additional ingredients near a moving blade. Occasionally, you may need to turn off your blender, remove the container from its base with lid in place, and give it a little shake to rearrange contents.

Or, as long as the blender is off, you may prefer to remove the lid and stir contents with a spoon.

EXPERIMENT FREELY! Don't be afraid to try out new flavor combinations and ingredients. You have nothing to lose and everything to gain, so mix it up in the kitchen (and in your blender, of course), and take your Smoothie passion to new heights!

NUMBER OF SERVINGS. Each Smoothie makes approximately 2 servings.

FRUIT AND VEGGIE FACTS

Before you dive head-first into your favorite Smoothie recipe, take a moment to brush up on these important fruit and veggie facts.

APPLE: Refreshingly crisp and satisfying, apples abound in autumn with flavors that range from cider sweet to lemony tart, and every combination in between. You can find many varieties of red, green, and golden apples any time of year, especially popular varieties like McIntosh, Granny Smith, and Golden Delicious. Apples are an excellent source of pectin, a soluble fiber that may help lower cholesterol. When selecting fresh apples, look for firm, colorful fruits without any bruised or wrinkled skin. For Smoothies, remove apple peel (if preferred) and core, cut into small chunks, and freeze if desired for extra frostiness. You can also get that sweet apple flavor from cider, juice, juice concentrates, and applesauce.

APRICOT: During those last few weeks of spring, run—don't walk—to your local grocery or specialty food store to find the sweetest, most delectable sun-ripened apricots. The golden-orange flesh of these plump little fruits is loaded with vitamin A and potassium. When dried, apricots provide fiber and beta-carotene, an important cancer-fighting antioxidant. Prepare fresh apricots by slicing in half, removing pits, and cutting into small chunks. Reconstitute dried apricots by covering in water or juice and soaking for at least an hour. Canned apricots and apricot nectar also make deliciously sweet additions to many Smoothies.

AVOCADO: The avocado is a natural in many vegetable-based Smoothies, with its buttery texture and mild, nutlike flavor. A great source of "good" monounsaturated fats and vitamin E, avocados are available year-round and range in color from bright green, like many smooth-skinned Florida varieties, to the black, wrinkled-skin types from California. Choose avocados that are soft to the touch, and prepare by slicing in half, twisting to remove the large center pit, and scooping out flesh. Use immediately or sprinkle with lemon juice to avoid discoloration due to oxidation.

BANANA: If bananas could talk, they might rightfully boast about being the most important ingredient in many Smoothies. With their creamy texture and sweet, mild

flavor, bananas, especially when frozen, put the "smooth" in Smoothie. Packed with potassium and fiber, bananas are nutritious and easy to digest, making them a great choice for kids. Buy golden yellow bananas without any visible bruises, and prepare for freezing, as I recommend, by removing peel and slicing. (One cup of sliced banana is approximately 1 whole banana.)

BEET: Beets make a bold statement in a Smoothie, in part for the sugary depth they add to other flavors, but most notably for the vision of loveliness they create in vibrant hues of pink and red. Find these antioxidant-rich root vegetables year-round, but especially in summertime, and choose those with firm, round shapes. Prepare beets for Smoothies by peeling and grating into small shreds. Beware: beets will also make a bold statement on anything they touch, like your fingers or shirt, so take precautions to avoid getting stained.

BLACKBERRY: Although you can often find frozen blackberries throughout the year, the very best time to get blackberries is when they're in season in mid to late summer. These purplish-black, juicy berries are a delicious blend of sweet and tart flavors, and are loaded with vitamin C and fiber. Blackberries also contain antioxidants that may play a role in reducing high blood pressure and the risk of cancer and heart disease. Select berries that are plump, firm, and dark purple in color, and sort in a bowl of cold water, removing any stems or imperfect berries. Though blackberry seeds are edible and nutritious, you may prefer to strain them if you're looking for an extra smooth blend.

BLUEBERRY: In late spring and early summer, fresh blueberries practically burst off their bushes into grocery stores and farmers' markets, tempting shoppers with their plump, juicy orbs of deep blue. A fine source of dietary fiber and one of the best sources of antioxidants, blueberries not only taste great but may help ward off cancer and other ailments associated with aging. Prepare blueberries by rinsing in a bowl of cold water, removing any stems or imperfect berries, and draining. Enjoy that great blueberry taste year-round using frozen blueberries, juice blends, juice concentrates, and sorbet.

CANTALOUPE: Most people love cantaloupe for its sweet orange flesh and refreshingly mild flavor, but what they may not know is that inside each one of these innocent-looking melons lies a nutritional powerhouse. While cantaloupe is very low in calories, it contains sky-high levels of beta-carotene, the plant pigment usually found in red, yellow, and orange fruits and vegetables known to play an important role in keeping the immune system healthy. Cantaloupe also delivers hefty doses of vitamin C and potassium, important for keeping body tissues strong. Find cantaloupes year-round but particularly in summer months. The netted skin of these round melons should be firm but give slightly under pressure. Prepare cantaloupes for Smoothies by slicing in half, removing seeds and rind, and cutting into small chunks. Cantaloupe, like other melons, can be frozen for Smoothies but tastes best when fresh.

CARROT: The crisp, sweet flavor of carrots comes alive in Smoothies, especially when paired with tart green apple or juicy orange. We've been told since childhood that carrots are good for our eyes, and they are, thanks to rich reserves of vitamin A that promote the growth and health of cells in our eyes and other body tissues. Find fresh carrot juice in the refrigerated section near the produce department of your grocery or specialty food store, or grate fresh, washed organic carrots right into the blender. As with other fruits and veggies, be sure to remove skin or peels if not organically grown.

CHERRY: There's something decadent about eating cherries, especially bowls full of deep, burgundy cherries, plucked fresh from the tree  and bursting with sticky-sweet, flavorful juice. Our bodies will thank us for indulging, however, since cherries contain vitamin C, fiber, and phytochemicals called anthocyanins that help strengthen collagen found in joints and connective tissues. Buy cherries by the bucketful when they're in season and fill your freezer for year-round delights. For Smoothies, place cherries in a bowl of cold water, and discard any that sink to the bottom of the bowl. Drain, remove stems and pits, and you're ready to blend! If you're crazy about cherries, find delicious cherry-flavored juices, juice concentrates, and sorbets year-round in most grocery or specialty food stores.

CRANBERRY: Nothing says autumn quite like the cranberry harvest, when acres of cranberry bogs are flooded and a sea of red cranberries floats to the surface. You can recreate your own mini harvest as you rinse and sort fresh cranberries, in season from early fall through winter. Though extremely tart and requiring added sweeteners, fresh cranberries contain respectable amounts of vitamin C and fiber, but of more importance, a substance known simply as "the cranberry factor" that helps prevent bladder infections by blocking bacteria from adhering to the bladder wall. For your convenience, canned cranberry sauces, juices, and juice concentrates are easy to use and make excellent additions to Smoothies.

CUCUMBER: We've all seen images of women at spas with pale green  cucumber rounds placed over their eyes in some sort of odd beauty ritual. Little did we know that cucumbers contain silica, a mineral that homeopathic medicine advocates believe strengthens connective tissue and improves the complexion. They certainly contain plentiful amounts of hydrating water. In Smoothies, cucumbers add a crisp, refreshing flavor that's sure to please. I prefer English hothouse varieties for their delicious flavor, but other organic, wax-free varieties work equally well. Prepare cucumbers by slicing in half, removing seeds, and chopping into small chunks.

DATE: You can enjoy the intensely sweet flavor of dates all year long, and reap the benefits of their fiber, potassium, and iron, a mineral that some women lack. Dates add a natural sweetness to Smoothies without overpowering other flavors, and just a few dates go a long way. Find full, chocolate-brown dates in the dried fruit section of your grocery or specialty food store, and prepare by removing pits and chopping into small pieces. For Smoothies, use these small bits as is, or, if you prefer, create a paste by blending them with a little water.

FIG: Fresh figs are a real treat, with their supple skin encasing densely sweet seed-filled centers. Because of their short shelf life, however, you will usually find figs dried. Either form offers excellent fiber and potassium, and makes for great Smoothies. Choose fresh figs that are plump, soft, and free from any visible scrapes, or buy pre-packaged dried figs. For Smoothies, remove fig stem, chop into small bits and use as is or create a paste by blending with water.

GRAPE: What's not to like about juicy sweet grapes? Whether they're yellowish-green, deep red, or burgundy, the sugar-sweet flavor of grapes enhances  Smoothies and adds a healthful heaping of vitamin C, potassium, and fiber. Most notably, red grapes contain a substance called resveratrol, which seems to have beneficial effects on the heart, and which is present in grape juice and juice concentrates. Select plump, firm, colorful bunches of seedless grapes and be sure to wash them thoroughly. Toss fresh grapes right into the blender, or freeze them first for an extra frosty treat. For added sweetness and extra iron, dried grapes or raisins also make tasty additions to Smoothies.

GRAPEFRUIT: Refreshingly tart and satisfyingly sweet, grapefruit delivers a powerful punch of flavor and nutrition, thanks in part to its hefty concentration of vitamin C, important for keeping the immune system and body tissues strong, and for aiding in iron absorption. Grapefruit also contains admirable levels of potassium and fiber; pink and red varieties contain beta-carotene. Grapefruit is available year-round but is best during winter and spring months. Choose full, round, heavy fruit and prepare by removing peel and as much of the inner white membrane as possible, unless you seek its extra-rich nutrients and don't mind the added bitterness. You simply can't go wrong using fresh grapefruit, or juice or juice concentrates, in Smoothies.

GUAVA: A stand-out star, the guava is considered by some to be the number one fruit when it comes to its total, nutritional package. Who would suspect that this pale yellow tropical fruit would contain just the right blend of nutrients and carotenoids—specifically beta-carotene, vitamin C, potassium, and fiber—making it superior to all others? Nutrition aside, the deliciously sweet and fruity flavor of guavas is hard to beat. Look for fresh guavas in fall and winter months in the tropical fruit section, or buy guava nectar all year long. As with other tropical fruits, which may have been treated with harmful pesticides, take special care to remove skin from fresh guavas before tossing guava flesh and edible seeds into Smoothies.

HONEYDEW: Like other melons, honeydew is an excellent choice for Smoothies because of its refreshingly mild flavor and smooth texture. Low in calories and high in nutrition, honeydew provides an excellent source of vitamin C and lutein, a phytochemical believed to reduce the risk of eye disorders and to help maintain good vision. You will find the sweetest honeydews during spring and summer months. Prepare by slicing in half, removing seeds and rind, and cutting into small chunks.

KIWIFRUIT: Everyone's crazy about kiwis, based on their prominence year-round. High in vitamin C and potassium, this egg-shaped tropical fruit has brown, fuzzy skin concealing a brilliant green, seed-speckled center. The sweet, lemon-tinged flavor of kiwis blends deliciously well in Smoothies, but since their tiny black seeds become bitter when ground in a blender, you should either remove them before blending or use a food processor. Always peel kiwis, as their skin may contain traces of harmful pesticides.

LEMON: When life gives you lemons, make a Smoothie, of course! The pleasantly sour flavor of lemon adds an extra kick to Smoothies, whether they're made with sweet fruits or mild-tasting vegetables. A rich source of vitamin C, chunks of fresh lemon work well in Smoothies, as do lemon juice, juice concentrate, sherbet, and sorbet. Find the juiciest lemons of the season during winter and spring months, and prepare for Smoothies by removing peel, seeds, and as much of the bitter white membrane as possible.

LIME: The tart taste of lime marries well with so many fruits and vegetables that it's practically  criminal not to use it. Like its sister citrus fruits, lime contains vitamin C, helpful in keeping gums healthy, warding off infection and aiding in iron absorption. Available year-round but best in winter and spring, limes should be firm but not hard, and a deep, vivid green. Prepare limes for Smoothies as you would prepare lemons. For a real treat, spike Smoothies with bottled lime juice, plain or sweetened, or sorbet.

MANGO: Golden orange mango flesh practically melts in your mouth with a peachy, tropical flavor that's hard to beat. Rich in vitamin C and beta-carotene, important for keeping the heart and immune system strong, mangoes create some of the most memorable Smoothies. You can find mangoes all year but should stock up during summer months when they're in season, freezing the extras. Look for ripe green mangoes, speckled with hints of red and yellow, and prepare for Smoothies by removing skin and shaving flesh away from large center pit. Mango juice, nectar, and sorbet also make wonderful Smoothies.

ORANGE: Tangy, sweet and delicious, oranges appeal to most everyone. They combine well with myriad flavors and deliver a healthful nutritional package to boot, complete with vitamin C and fiber. Oranges also contain folate, essential for making new body cells. Orange season spans through winter and spring, although you can find the ever-present orange just about anytime. Use orange juice, juice concentrate, or sherbet in Smoothies, or prepare fresh oranges by removing peel and white membrane, and seeds if you're not using a seedless variety. Tangerines, closely related to oranges but slightly more tart, are also readily available and make outstanding Smoothies.

PAPAYA: If you haven't tasted papaya, you're truly missing out on one of nature's finest creations. Papaya flesh is a lovely orange-pink color and tastes like peach-infused melon. Nutritionists sing its praises, for a single papaya contains a bounty of vitamin C, folate, potassium, and fiber. Find deep yellow pear-shaped papayas with other tropical fruits in your grocery store, especially during spring and summer months. Prepare much as you would a melon by slicing in half, removing seeds, and either scooping or slicing flesh away from skin. Papaya juice or nectar, usually available at your grocery or specialty store, deliver great flavor in just about any fruit blend.

PASSION FRUIT: I don't know about you, but just the name of this enticing fruit strands me on a tropical island with nothing but exotic fruit and very helpful, well-toned rescuers. At home, however, the best way to create your own tropical heat is by adding tangy sweet passion fruit juice or sorbet (from a grocery or specialty food store) to a Smoothie. Fresh passion fruits resemble wrinkled, reddish-purple plums, and, when sliced in half, reveal a startling, fleshy, seeded center. Unlike melons, the seeded, gelatinous core of passion fruits, loaded with vitamin C and fiber, is what you eat, and don't discard. In Smoothies, however, I find the seeds add a bit too much texture for my taste, and I prefer the smooth creaminess of juice or sorbet.

PEACH: Summertime to many folks means big baskets of reddish-yellow peaches, plucked fresh from the tree when heavy with sweet, natural juices. There's nothing like a peach Smoothie to cool you off on a hot summer day, not to mention the dose of vitamin C and beta-carotene it provides. Buy fresh peaches all summer long and prepare by removing skin (if peaches are not organic), slicing in half, discarding pit, and cutting into small chunks. Canned peaches, peach nectar, and sorbet are readily available year-round and make great Smoothies.

PEAR: Many varieties of fresh pears are available year-round, though my favorite, the Bartlett pear, peaks in late summer and early autumn with a satisfyingly sweet taste all its own. The key to pears is eating them when they're perfectly ripe, sometimes challenging because they're picked green and hard, often the way you find them at the store. Ripen pears at home by placing them in a closed brown paper bag with an apple or banana

thrown in to speed the process with the chemicals they release while ripening. A few days will do the trick; then simply peel (if not organic), remove core, and cut into chunks. For Smoothies you may also use canned pears, juice, and nectar.

PINEAPPLE: Recognized worldwide as a symbol of hospitality, pineapples make incredibly flavorful, delicious Smoothies that'll leave you begging for more. Rich in vitamin C and bromelain, a substance believed to have anti-inflammatory properties, fresh pineapples are available year-round, though you'll find the best in winter and spring months. To assess ripeness, grasp pineapple by one of its long, pointed leaves

 and lift. Leaves will come off easily from very ripe pineapples. As with other fruits, use your senses to find a sweet smelling pineapple that gives slightly when pressed.

Prepare by removing leaves, skin, and center core, and cutting into chunks. Toss chunks right into the blender. You may substitute canned pineapple, juice, and juice concentrate for equally fantastic Smoothies.

PLUM: On hazy summer days long ago, my friends and I would pick dozens of green, yellow, and purple plums from the trees in their backyard, discussing the merits of each variety between every juicy bite. As you may know, they're all good, except perhaps when they're under-ripe and exceedingly sour. Find the most colorful array of sweet-tart plums during summer months, and prepare for Smoothies by slicing in half, removing center pit, and cutting into chunks. Plums are a good source of vitamin C and phytochemicals called phenolics, believed to slow some effects of aging. When dried into prunes, plums deliver excellent fiber and outstanding taste. Just don't overdo it, as a few prunes or a cup of prune juice go a long way.

PUMPKIN: If you like pumpkin pie and you care about your health, you'll be thrilled with the rich, creamy taste of Smoothies made with canned pumpkin, as well as with the powerful blast of vitamin A you'll receive. The beta-carotene in pumpkins may play an important role in reducing cancer and heart disease, so you have everything to gain by giving this squash a go. Find fresh pumpkins in October, and canned pumpkin year-round near other canned fruits in your local grocery store.

RASPBERRY: Brilliant pink-red raspberries create beautiful blends with outstanding flavor. They're also nutritious, with a mega  dose of vitamin C and anthocyanins, the phytochemicals believed to lower blood pressure and improve circulation. Buy frozen raspberries all year long or, during summer months, select the reddest, plumpest raspberries you can find. Prepare by sorting berries in a bowl of cold water, removing any stems or imperfect berries, and draining. Freeze if desired. Other raspberry products make great additions to Smoothies, including raspberry juice, juice concentrate, sherbet, and sorbet.

RED BELL PEPPER: Red bell pepper is one of my favorite additions to many vegetable-based Smoothies, with its tangy sweet flesh and deep, red color. It's also an excellent source of beta-carotene and vitamin C, important for keeping the immune system healthy and for warding off disease. Red bell peppers are available year-round, although you will find the best selection when they're in season throughout the summer. Choose firm peppers without any scrapes or bruises. Prepare by slicing in half, removing seeds and white membrane, and cutting into small chunks.

STRAWBERRY: Like the first daffodils of the season, strawberries scream springtime, rousing us from our winter slumber with their bold, beautiful color. Load up on these sweet, delicious red berries while you can, knowing that you can safely freeze any excess. Like other berries, strawberries are rich in vitamin C and antioxidants, so eat heartily and enjoy. You will love the punch a few fresh strawberries add to Smoothies, and you can also find that sweet strawberry goodness in strawberry juice blends, concentrates, sherbet, sorbet, and ice cream.

TOMATO: The tale of the tomato is a tragic one: born a fruit (berry, actually); perceived a vegetable (oh the horror); sold for sauce; and squashed. But that's just one perspective. We have juicy, sun-ripened veggie-fruits available year-round, especially during spring and summer months, and aisles filled

with canned toma-
toes. And nutrition-
ally speaking, it's the
canned tomatoes

and sauces that serve us best—men in par-
ticular—because of a phytochemical called
lycopene that may reduce the risk of
prostate cancer and protect against heart
attacks and strokes. Whatever form you
choose, whether it's farm stand fresh or
drinkable and canned, you will find a
favorite in tomato-based Smoothies.

WATERMELON: Another noteworthy star,
the watermelon packs a mighty nutritional
punch for a fruit comprised largely of water
(over 90%!). In addition to its vitamin C
and respectable amounts of fiber and potassium, the watermelon is loaded with beta-
carotene that may help ward off illness and
even some kinds of cancer. Drinking a
watermelon Smoothie, refreshingly sweet
and beautifully pink, will cool you off on

summer's hottest days and hydrate your body with nutrient-rich water. Find fresh watermelons year-round but particularly during spring and summer months. Seedless varieties work best in Smoothies.

OTHER IMPORTANT INGREDIENTS

JUICES AND NECTARS: You will find an impressive array of fruit juices, nectars, and juice blends lining store shelves these days, and you need only select your favorite combinations and start blending. Frozen juice concentrates and all-juice popsicles work well as ice cold sweeteners, but my favorite trick is freezing juices or nectars in ice cube trays and adding crushed cubes to Smoothies.

DAIRY PRODUCTS: Dairy products make excellent binders in Smoothies, particularly foods like milk, yogurt, and frozen yogurt that spike the creaminess factor while adding calcium and vitamin D for strong bones and teeth. If you like yogurt in your

Smoothies, I suggest you purchase individual yogurts in your favorite flavors and pop them in the freezer, ready to blend when you are. (Commercial frozen yogurt may also be used, in the same quantity called for in a recipe.) Buttermilk, sherbet, and ice cream also make fabulously rich Smoothies. Most of my recipes call for low-fat or non-fat dairy products though, naturally, you are free to substitute the varieties of your choice.

DAIRY ALTERNATIVES: A bounty of dairy alternatives, ideal for Smoothies, awaits you in grocery and specialty food stores. I love the mellow nuttiness of almond milk, the creaminess of soft silken tofu, and the subtle sweetness of vanilla soy milk. The possibilities are limitless when you're looking to add liquid and/or texture to help bind your Smoothie ingredients together. Other favorites include coconut milk, rice milk, sorbet, and tea.

NUTS, SEEDS, AND GRAINS: Bolster the nutritional content of your favorite Smoothie by adding a few nuts, seeds, or grains to the mix. Nuts and nut butters, such as almond, cashew, and peanut, add excellent protein and texture to Smoothies, not to mention unbeatable flavor. Many choose to add sesame seeds, tahini, or flaxseed oil to their Smoothies, in part for their subtle, nutty taste but also for health reasons. Just a tablespoon of wheat germ, my personal favorite, supplies vitamin E and folic acid, and adds great texture and flavor. Other possibilities include rolled oats, granola, or shredded sweetened or unsweetened coconut.

SWEETENERS: My Smoothie sweetener of choice is honey, since it combines well with most ingredients and doesn't overpower other flavors. Fruit juice concentrate, all-fruit popsicles, and maple syrup are other favorites. Some natural sweeteners are brown rice syrup and barley malt.

NUTRITIONAL SUPPLEMENTS: Many Smoothie shops offer people the option of adding various health-minded supplements to their blends, with some of the most popular being protein powder, brewer's yeast, and bee pollen. If this is something you choose to do, go right ahead. Be aware, however, that some supplements—particularly brewer's yeast—will alter the taste of your Smoothie.

smoothies for any time

BREAKFAST BLENDS

LIQUID LUNCHES

AFTERNOON DELIGHTS

EVENING ELIXIRS

breakfast
blends...

Doubtless God could have made a better
berry, but doubtless God never did.

WILLIAM BUTLER,
DESCRIBING THE STRAWBERRY

RISE 'N RASPBERRY

You can't go wrong with this tangy-sweet, berry blend. Add 1 table-spoon rolled oats or wheat germ for added texture and taste.

1 cup chilled orange juice
1/2 cup non-fat raspberry yogurt
1/2 frozen banana
1-1/2 cups frozen raspberries

Pour orange juice into blender and add yogurt, banana, and raspberries. Blend at high speed until smooth.

47

MORNING MANGO

The perfect breakfast for mango lovers!

1 cup chilled mango juice
3/4 cup low-fat lemon yogurt
1/2 frozen banana
1 cup frozen mango chunks

Pour mango juice into blender and add yogurt, banana, and mango. Blend at high speed until smooth.

STRAWBERRY SUNRISE

If every day included a Strawberry Sunrise, the world would be a much happier place.

1 cup chilled orange juice
1/2 cup non-fat vanilla yogurt
1/2 frozen banana
1 tablespoon wheat germ
1 cup frozen strawberries
1 tablespoon honey (optional)

Pour orange juice into blender and add yogurt, banana, wheat germ, and strawberries. Blend at high speed until smooth. For extra sweetness, add 1 tablespoon honey.

BLUEBERRY BEGINNINGS

You'll feel anything but blue after enjoying this delicious blend!

1 cup chilled white grape juice
1/2 cup low-fat blueberry yogurt
1/2 frozen banana
1 cup frozen blueberries

Pour white grape juice into blender and add yogurt, banana, and blueberries. Blend at high speed until smooth.

DELICIOUS DAYBREAK

Start your day off right with this deliciously creamy fruit blend!

1 cup chilled orange juice
1/2 cup non-fat vanilla yogurt
1/2 cup frozen strawberries
1/2 cup cantaloupe chunks
1 frozen banana
1 tablespoon granola (optional)

Pour orange juice into blender and add yogurt, strawberries, and cantaloupe. Pulse until combined, then add banana and blend at high speed until smooth. Add granola for more fiber and texture.

EARLY APPLE

A sweet, nutritious way to start your day!

1 cup chilled pear nectar
1/2 cup applesauce
4 frozen pitted prunes, chopped
1 frozen banana
3 ice cubes, crushed

Pour pear nectar into blender and add applesauce, prunes, banana, and crushed ice. Blend at high speed until smooth.

SUNSHINY CITRUS

Let the sunshine in with this blast of citrus goodness.

1/2 cup chilled orange juice
1/2 cup non-fat vanilla yogurt
1 cup orange segments
1/2 cup grapefruit segments
1 tablespoon wheat germ
6 frozen pineapple juice cubes, crushed
1 to 2 tablespoons honey (optional)

Pour orange juice into blender and add yogurt, oranges, grapefruit, and wheat germ. Pulse until combined, then add crushed pineapple juice cubes and blend at high speed until smooth. Add honey for extra sweetness, if desired.

GOOD MORNING GUAVA

For a taste of the tropics try this scrumptious Smoothie.

1 cup chilled guava nectar
1/2 cup low-fat lemon yogurt
1/2 cup canned or fresh pineapple chunks
1/2 frozen banana
3 ice cubes, crushed
2 tablespoons coconut milk (optional)

Pour guava nectar into blender and add yogurt, pineapple, banana, and crushed ice. Blend at high speed until smooth.

To really wake up in the tropics, add coconut milk.

liquid
lunches...

I believe the medicine chest
of the twenty-first century
is in the produce department!

LYNDA RESNICK

MIDDAY MELON

If you can't take a shower midway through your day, this pure and delicious Smoothie may leave you feeling just as refreshed.

1 cup chilled orange juice
1 cup cantaloupe chunks
1/2 cup honeydew chunks
1/2 cup lemon sorbet
3 ice cubes, crushed

Pour orange juice into blender and add cantaloupe, honeydew, sorbet, and crushed ice. Blend at high speed until smooth.

PEACHY EATS

Feel "peachy" for the rest of the day after this satisfyingly fruity and nutritious blend.

1/2 cup chilled papaya nectar
1/2 cup chilled vanilla soy milk
1-1/2 cups frozen peach chunks
1/4 cup soft silken tofu
1/2 cup peach sorbet
1 teaspoon vanilla extract
1 to 2 tablespoons honey (optional)

Pour papaya nectar and vanilla soy milk into blender and add peaches, tofu, sorbet, and vanilla extract. Alternate blending between high and low speeds until smooth. Add honey when you feel the need for a punch of sweetness.

LUNCH LIME

Refreshingly tart and delicious, this mint green Smoothie is sure to please.

1 cup chilled white grape juice
2 tablespoons fresh lime juice
1/2 cup seeded cucumber chunks
1/2 cup lime sorbet
1 cup frozen seedless green grapes

Pour white grape juice and lime juice into blender and add cucumbers, sorbet, and grapes. Blend at high speed until smooth.

GRAPE ON THE GO

A sweet, delicious, and beautifully hued purple Smoothie.

1 cup chilled grape juice
1/2 cup frozen non-fat vanilla yogurt
1 cup frozen red seedless grapes
1/2 cup blueberries

Pour grape juice into blender and add yogurt, grapes, and blueberries. Blend at high speed until smooth.

NUTTY NOONER

When you need some added "oomph" in your day, try this protein-rich, nutty, sweet Smoothie!

1 cup chilled vanilla soy milk
2 tablespoons peanut butter
6 chopped pitted dates, frozen
1-1/2 frozen bananas

Pour vanilla soy milk into blender and add peanut butter, dates, and bananas. Blend at high speed until smooth.

OAT TO LUNCH

The quintessential meal-in-a-glass, this tasty blend of fruit flavors pairs perfectly with the satisfying heartiness of oats.

1 cup chilled apple juice
1/2 cup non-fat raspberry yogurt
1 cup frozen strawberries
1/2 frozen banana
2 tablespoons uncooked, quick rolled oats

Pour apple juice into blender and add yogurt, strawberries, banana, and rolled oats. Blend at high speed until smooth.

CHERRY IN A HURRY

You can't help but smile when you taste this creamy cherry blend.

1 cup chilled apple juice
1/2 cup non-fat black cherry yogurt
1/2 frozen banana
1-1/2 cups frozen pitted cherries

Pour apple juice into blender and add yogurt, banana, and cherries. Blend at high speed until smooth.

TOMATOES AT TWELVE

You will love the flavor and nutrition of this tomato blend.

1 cup canned tomatoes with juice
1/2 cup non-fat plain yogurt
1 cup chopped, seeded cucumber chunks
1 teaspoon Worcestershire sauce
1/2 teaspoon celery salt
Dash Tabasco sauce
1 teaspoon fresh lemon juice
6 crushed frozen carrot juice cubes

Pour tomatoes and juice, yogurt, cucumber, spices, and lemon juice into blender and blend until combined. Add crushed carrot juice cubes and blend at high speed until smooth.

afternoon
delights...

Tomatoes are lusty enough, yet there
runs through tomatoes an undercurrent
of frivolity. Beets are deadly serious.

TOM ROBBINS

CHAI TIME

Tea time will never be the same after you've tried this deliciously creamy, spiced Smoothie!

1/2 cup chilled non-fat milk
1 cup chilled strong black tea
1/2 cup non-fat vanilla frozen yogurt
2 tablespoons honey
1 frozen banana
1/4 teaspoon cinnamon
1/4 teaspoon clove
1/4 teaspoon ginger
3 ice cubes, crushed

Pour milk and tea into blender and add yogurt, honey, banana, and spices. Blend at high speed until smooth; add crushed ice and blend until smooth.

PERK-ME-UP PAPAYA

A knock-out fruit punch that'll set you right for the rest of the day!

1 cup chilled orange juice
1 cup papaya chunks
1/2 cup frozen strawberries
1 frozen banana

Pour orange juice into blender and add papaya, strawberries, and banana. Blend at high speed until smooth.

BERRY BREAK

You won't be able to hide your delight (and purple-stained lips) after this berry-rich blend!

1 cup chilled grape juice
3/4 cup frozen blackberries
3/4 cup frozen blueberries

Pour grape juice into blender and add blackberries and blueberries. Blend at high speed until smooth.

ESPRESSO BOOST

This deep, dark, and delicious Smoothie will quickly become part of your daily ritual.

1/2 cup chilled espresso
1/2 cup chilled non-fat milk
1 frozen banana
3/4 cup chocolate sorbet
3 ice cubes, crushed

Pour espresso and milk into blender and add banana, sorbet, and crushed ice. Blend at high speed until smooth.

JAVA JOLT

Transform your afternoon cup of coffee into a creamy dream with this frosty blend!

1 cup chilled strong black coffee
1 frozen banana
3/4 cup frozen non-fat vanilla yogurt
1/4 teaspoon cinnamon

Pour coffee into blender and add banana, yogurt, and cinnamon. Blend at high speed until smooth.

RASPBERRY REFRESHER

A most invigorating raspberry
Smoothie with just a hint of lime!

1 cup chilled white grape juice
1 cup frozen raspberries
1/2 cup watermelon chunks
1 tablespoon fresh lime juice
3 ice cubes, crushed

Pour white grape juice into blender and add
raspberries, watermelon, lime juice, and
crushed ice. Blend at high speed until
smooth.

LEMON LIFT

Pucker up for this delightfully tart Smoothie!

2 tablespoons fresh lemon juice
1 cup chilled pineapple juice
1 cup canned or fresh pineapple chunks
3/4 cup lemon sherbet
3 ice cubes, crushed

Pour lemon juice and pineapple juice into blender and add pineapple, sherbet, and crushed ice. Blend at high speed until smooth.

evening
elixirs...

Forget love...I'd rather fall in chocolate!

AUTHOR UNKNOWN

CALL FOR CHOCOLATE

Richly flavored chocolate Smoothie with a banana-berry twist!

1 cup chilled chocolate soy milk
1 frozen banana
1/2 cup frozen raspberries
1/2 cup chocolate sorbet

Pour chocolate soy milk into blender and add banana, raspberries, and sorbet. Blend at high speed until smooth.

KIWI COCKTAIL

Shift gears from work to play with this tropical treat.

1 cup chilled guava nectar
2 medium kiwis, peeled and cut into chunks
1 tablespoon fresh lime juice
6 ice cubes, crushed

Pour guava nectar into food processor and add kiwis, lime juice, and crushed ice. Pulse until smooth.

AFTER HOURS PASSION

Your long, hard day will be a distant memory after one sip of this exotic delight. Add some reggae and a sarong to the mix and end your day in Jamaica!

1 cup chilled passion fruit juice
1/2 frozen banana
1/2 cup canned or fresh pineapple chunks
1/2 cup passion fruit sorbet
2 tablespoons coconut milk
3 ice cubes, crushed

Pour passion fruit juice into blender and add banana, pineapple, sorbet, coconut milk, and crushed ice. Blend at high speed until smooth.

ORANGE SUNSET

Watch the sun set while drinking your own! This beautiful orange-red Smoothie will set you afire with the sweetness of mangoes and cherries coupled with lemony citrus.

1 cup chilled orange juice
1 tablespoon fresh lemon juice
1 cup frozen mango chunks
1/2 cup frozen pitted cherries

Pour orange juice and lemon juice into blender and add mango and cherries. Blend at high speed until smooth.

CRAN-APPLE COOL DOWN

Kick off your shoes with this flavorful tart-sweet blend!

1 cup chilled cranberry juice cocktail
1/2 cup whole berry cranberry sauce
3 ice cubes, crushed
1 cup frozen apple chunks

Pour cranberry juice cocktail into blender and add cranberry sauce, crushed ice, and apple chunks. Blend at high speed until smooth.

STARRY, STARRY STRAWBERRY

Count every star in the sky while savoring the flavors of strawberry, mango, banana, and guava.

1 cup chilled guava nectar
1 cup frozen strawberries
1/2 cup mango chunks
1/2 frozen banana

Pour guava nectar into blender and add strawberries, mango, and banana. Blend at high speed until smooth.

ALMOND MOON

Too much just isn't enough of this
scrumptious almond Smoothie.
If you're a real nut, garnish with
slivered almonds or toss some
into the mix!

1 cup chilled almond milk
3/4 cup frozen non-fat vanilla yogurt
2 tablespoons almond butter
1/2 teaspoon almond extract
1-1/2 frozen bananas

Pour almond milk into blender and add
yogurt, almond butter, almond extract, and
bananas. Blend at high speed until smooth.

BEDTIME BANANA

So simple but simply delicious!

1 cup chilled non-fat milk
3/4 cup frozen low-fat banana yogurt
1 tablespoon maple syrup
3 ice cubes, crushed
1-1/2 frozen bananas

Pour milk into blender and add yogurt, maple syrup, crushed ice, and bananas. Blend at high speed until smooth.

SWEET BERRY DREAMS

Try this creamy berry Smoothie before bedtime and you'll be smiling all night.

1 cup chilled vanilla soy milk
1/2 cup frozen non-fat vanilla yogurt
1 cup frozen raspberries
1/2 cup frozen strawberries

Pour soy milk into blender and add yogurt, raspberries, and strawberries. Blend at high speed until smooth.

ARM CHAIR PEAR

You'll know you're home when you settle into your favorite chair with this mellow pleaser.

1 cup chilled pear nectar
1/2 cup canned pears, drained
1/2 cup frozen honeydew chunks
1/2 cup lemon sherbet

Pour pear nectar into blender and add pears, honeydew, and lemon sherbet. Blend at high speed until smooth.

smoothies by
the season

SPRING SIPPERS

SUMMER SHAKES

FALL FROSTIES

WINTER FREEZES

spring sippers...

And every day that I've been good,
I get an orange after food.

ROBERT LOUIS STEVENSON

CITRUS CROCUS

Wake up your taste buds with this tart ginger Smoothie!

1 cup chilled orange juice
2 tablespoons fresh lemon juice
3/4 cup lime sorbet
1 tablespoon fresh, grated ginger
6 ice cubes, crushed
1 to 2 tablespoons honey (optional)

Pour orange juice and lemon juice into blender and add sorbet, ginger, and crushed ice. Blend at high speed until smooth. Add honey for extra sweetness, if desired.

STRAWBERRY PATCH SPLENDOR

A strawberry lover's delight!

1 cup chilled non-fat milk
1/2 cup strawberry sorbet
1-1/2 cups frozen strawberries
1/2 frozen banana

Pour milk into blender and add sorbet, strawberries, and banana. Blend at high speed until smooth.

BLUEBERRY BOUQUET

You will love this delicious blend of two of spring's finest fruits with the sweet tang of mango.

1 cup chilled mango juice
1 cup frozen blueberries
1/2 cup frozen strawberries
3 ice cubes, crushed

Pour mango juice into blender and add blueberries, strawberries, and crushed ice. Blend at high speed until smooth.

APRICOT AWAKENING

If you love the taste of apricots, this is the Smoothie for you!

1 cup chilled apricot nectar
1/2 cup frozen non-fat vanilla yogurt
1 cup fresh or canned apricot chunks
3 ice cubes, crushed

Pour apricot nectar into blender and add yogurt, apricots, and crushed ice. Blend at high speed until smooth.

HOME RUN HONEYDEW

Go extra innings with this minty green winner!

1-1/2 cups honeydew chunks
1 tablespoon fresh lime juice
3/4 cup lime sorbet
1 teaspoon fresh mint
6 ice cubes, crushed

Add honeydew, lime juice, sorbet, and mint to blender and blend at high speed until smooth. Add crushed ice and continue blending until smooth.

TEE TIME LEMON

At home or at play you'll be shouting for more of this Smoothie.

1 cup chilled white grape juice
2 tablespoons fresh lemon juice
3/4 cup lemon sorbet
2 tablespoons honey
6 ice cubes, crushed

Pour white grape juice and lemon juice into blender and add sorbet, honey, and crushed ice. Blend at high speed until smooth.

GRAND SLAM GRAPE

Take me out to the ball game with one of these delicious grape Smoothies!

1 cup chilled peach nectar
1 cup frozen red grapes
1/2 cup frozen green grapes
3 ice cubes, crushed

Pour peach nectar into blender and add grapes and crushed ice. Blend at high speed until smooth.

RAINY DAY BLUES

The blue-violet color of this creamy, dreamy Smoothie would be enough to scare away the clouds, but its sweet, fruity flavor really lets the sun shine through!

1 cup blueberry juice blend
1/2 cup frozen non-fat vanilla yogurt
1 cup drained, canned peaches
1 cup frozen blueberries

Pour blueberry juice into blender and add yogurt, peaches, and blueberries. Blend at high speed until smooth.

summer
shakes...

When one has tasted watermelons
one knows what angels eat.

MARK TWAIN

CANTALOUPE CROQUET

Whether it's badminton, horseshoes, or croquet, you can't lose with this summertime Smoothie.

1 cup chilled pineapple juice
1 cup cantaloupe chunks
1/2 frozen banana
1/2 cup orange sherbet

Pour pineapple juice into blender and add cantaloupe, banana, and sherbet. Blend at high speed until smooth.

PEACHY PICNIC

Enough to share, even if you don't want to!

1 cup chilled orange juice
1/2 cup non-fat peach yogurt
1 cup frozen peach chunks
1/2 cup frozen raspberries
1/2 frozen banana

Pour orange juice into blender and add yogurt, peaches, raspberries, and banana. Blend at high speed until smooth.

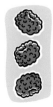

RELAXING RASPBERRY

Cool down with this sweet raspberry
Smoothie while you're hanging out
in the hammock.

1 cup chilled apple juice
1-1/2 cups raspberries
1/2 frozen banana
2 tablespoons frozen raspberry juice
  concentrate
1 cup crushed ice

Pour apple juice into blender and add raspberries, banana, raspberry juice concentrate,
and crushed ice. Blend at high speed until
smooth.

PLUM-CHERRY COOLER

A plum delicious way to turn down the heat on summer's hottest days!

1 cup chilled cranberry juice
1 cup plum chunks
1/2 cup frozen pitted dark cherries
1/2 cup frozen low-fat black cherry yogurt

Pour cranberry juice into blender and add plums, cherries, and yogurt. Blend at high speed until smooth.

BLACKBERRY BIKE RIDE

Don't feel guilty about downing this deep purple, luscious Smoothie. It's not as if you climbed over the fence and swiped your neighbor's black-berries—or did you?

1 cup chilled apricot nectar
1 teaspoon fresh lemon juice
1 cup frozen blackberries
1/2 cup non-fat blackberry yogurt
3 ice cubes, crushed

Pour apricot nectar and lemon juice into blender and add blackberries, yogurt, and crushed ice. Blend at high speed until smooth.

SKINNY CARROT DIPPER

Try it. You'll like it. It's incredibly refreshing. (Skinny dipping is, too!)

3/4 cup chilled buttermilk
1 cup seeded cucumber chunks
1 tablespoon fresh parsley
6 frozen carrot juice cubes, crushed
1 tablespoon fresh lemon juice
3 ice cubes, crushed

Pour buttermilk into blender and add cucumbers, parsley, crushed carrot juice cubes, and lemon juice. Blend at high speed until smooth, then add crushed ice and continue blending until smooth.

GAME, SET, MANGO

You'll be serving all aces just knowing this minty mango treat awaits
you off the court. If your game has
soured, sweeten up this Smoothie
with honey.

1 cup chilled apricot nectar
1-1/2 cups frozen mango chunks
1 tablespoon fresh mint
6 ice cubes, crushed
1 to 2 tablespoons honey (optional)

Pour apricot nectar into blender and add
mango, mint, and crushed ice. Blend at high
speed until smooth.

WATERMELON SPLASH

You'll want to dive right into this refreshing watermelon Smoothie and slurp up every sweet, basil-berry drop.

1-1/2 cups watermelon chunks
1/2 cup frozen strawberries
1/2 cup strawberry sorbet
1 teaspoon fresh lime juice
1 teaspoon fresh basil

Add all ingredients to blender and pulse until combined. Then blend at high speed until smooth.

fall frosties...

Comfort me with apples:
for I am sick of love.

THE SONG OF SOLOMON 2:5

CRANBERRY CHILLER

A great choice for Halloween night!

1 cup chilled cranberry juice cocktail
1/2 cup fresh cranberries
1 cup drained canned pears
1/4 cup frozen raspberry juice concentrate
3 ice cubes, crushed

Pour cranberry juice cocktail into blender and add cranberries, pears, raspberry juice concentrate, and crushed ice. Blend at high speed until smooth.

TOUCHDOWN APPLE

This refreshing apple Smoothie scores big on flavor with its winning combination of apple, banana, and pineapple.

1 cup chilled apple juice
3/4 cup applesauce
1/2 cup canned pineapple chunks
1/2 frozen banana
6 ice cubes, crushed

Pour apple juice into blender and add applesauce, pineapple, banana, and crushed ice. Blend at high speed until smooth.

HOMECOMING DATE

A sweet charmer, just like your date should be.

1 cup chilled vanilla soy milk
6 pitted dates, chopped
1 frozen banana
3/4 cup frozen non-fat vanilla yogurt
1 tablespoon honey

Pour vanilla soy milk into blender and add dates, banana, yogurt, and honey. Blend at high speed until smooth.

HARVEST MIXER

Like splendid fall foliage, this colorful array of fruit flavors celebrates
the season in all its glory.

1 cup chilled pear nectar
1/2 cup chilled cranberry juice
1 cup frozen pear chunks
2 tablespoons frozen apple juice concentrate
6 ice cubes, crushed

Pour pear nectar and cranberry juice into
blender and add pear, apple juice concentrate, and crushed ice. Blend at high speed
until smooth.

PEAR-APPLE CRISPER

Post pumpkin-picking and before
the hay ride, try this sweet, saucy
treat to get you in the mood!

1 cup chilled pear nectar
1 cup canned pears with juice
1/2 cup applesauce
1 frozen banana
1 tablespoon raisins
3 ice cubes, crushed

Pour pear nectar into blender and add pears,
applesauce, banana, raisins, and crushed ice.
Blend at high speed until smooth.

FIRESIDE FIGGY

The perfect Smoothie for cuddling up by the fire on chilly autumn nights!

1 cup chilled non-fat milk
4 dried figs rehydrated in 1/2 cup water
1 frozen banana
3/4 cup frozen non-fat vanilla yogurt
2 tablespoons maple syrup
3 ice cubes, crushed

Pour milk into blender and add figs, banana, yogurt, maple syrup, and crushed ice. Blend at high speed until smooth.

ICY SPICY CIDER

Apple pie à la mode—in a glass!

1 cup chilled apple cider
1/2 cup applesauce
1/2 cup frozen non-fat vanilla yogurt
1/2 teaspoon cinnamon
3 ice cubes, crushed

Pour apple cider into blender and add apple-sauce, yogurt, cinnamon, and crushed ice. Blend at high speed until smooth.

PUMPKIN PIE PLEASER

If you love pumpkin pie and pumpkin ice cream, this delicious Smoothie happily marries the two.

1 cup chilled vanilla soy milk
1 cup canned pumpkin
1/2 cup frozen non-fat vanilla yogurt
2 tablespoons honey
1 teaspoon pumpkin pie spice
3 ice cubes, crushed

Pour soy milk into blender and add pumpkin, yogurt, honey, spice, and crushed ice. Blend at high speed until smooth.

winter
freezes...

There is a lot more juice in a
grapefruit than meets the eye.

AUTHOR UNKNOWN

PINEAPPLE-CITRUS SLUSH

Here's a Smoothie to chase away the winter blues.

1 cup pineapple juice
1 cup canned or fresh pineapple chunks
1/2 cup pink grapefruit segments
1/2 cup orange sherbet
6 ice cubes, crushed

Pour pineapple juice into blender and add pineapple, grapefruit, sherbet, and crushed ice. Blend at high speed until smooth.

GRAPEFRUIT HAIL

All hail the grapefruit!

1 cup chilled apple juice
1 cup pink grapefruit segments
1/2 cup lemon sorbet
3 ice cubes, crushed

Pour apple juice into blender and add grapefruit, sorbet, and crushed ice. Blend at high speed until smooth.

BANANA BLIZZARD

Get lost in this banana blizzard and find yourself in a creamy vanilla paradise!

1 cup chilled non-fat milk
1-1/2 frozen bananas
3/4 cup non-fat vanilla yogurt
1 teaspoon vanilla extract
2 tablespoons honey

Pour milk into blender and add bananas, yogurt, vanilla extract, and honey. Blend at high speed until smooth.

HOLIDAY ORANGE

Feel the holiday spirit with this delicious Smoothie, spiced like a pomander orange and iced with creamy eggnog.

1 cup eggnog
1 cup canned mandarin oranges with juice
1 frozen banana
1/2 cup orange sherbet
1/2 teaspoon cinnamon
3 ice cubes, crushed

Pour eggnog into blender and add mandarin oranges, banana, sherbet, cinnamon, and crushed ice. Blend at high speed until smooth.

EXTREME SKIWI

You'll feel like a snow bunny when you drink this Smoothie.

1 cup chilled passion fruit juice
2 medium kiwis, peeled and cut into chunks
1 frozen banana
1/2 cup frozen non-fat vanilla yogurt

Pour passion fruit juice into food processor and add kiwis, banana, and yogurt. Pulse until smooth.

TANGERINE WARMER

A burst of warm sunshine on a dark, cold winter day!

1 cup fresh tangerine juice
1 cup drained, canned mandarin oranges
1/2 cup peach sorbet
1/2 cup frozen non-fat vanilla yogurt

Pour tangerine juice into blender and add mandarin oranges, sorbet, and yogurt. Blend at high speed until smooth.

SKI LODGE LIME

Relax by the fire with this perfect blend of sweet and tart.

1 cup chilled white grape juice
2 tablespoons fresh lime juice
3/4 cup lemon sherbet
1/4 cup frozen raspberry juice concentrate
6 ice cubes, crushed

Pour white grape juice and lime juice into blender and add sherbet, raspberry juice concentrate, and crushed ice. Blend at high speed until smooth.

TROPICAL GETAWAY

Aloha and welcome to paradise!
Unpack your suitcase, add some
shredded, sweetened coconut to
this Smoothie, and stay as long
as you like.

1/2 cup orange juice
1/2 cup coconut milk
1 cup canned or cut-up fresh pineapple
1 frozen banana
1/2 cup frozen low-fat vanilla yogurt
Shredded sweetened coconut

Pour orange juice and coconut milk into
blender and add pineapple, banana, and
yogurt. Blend at high speed until smooth.
Garnish with shredded coconut.

CHERRY VALENTINE

Surprise your valentine with this creamy, cherry-chocolate smoothie and say "Be Mine" in the smoothest of ways!

1 cup chilled black cherry juice
1/2 cup chilled chocolate soy milk
3/4 cup frozen black cherry yogurt
1 to 2 tablespoons sweetened cocoa powder
  (optional)

Pour black cherry juice and chocolate soy milk into blender, add frozen yogurt, and blend at high speed until smooth. For an extra chocolaty treat, add sweetened cocoa powder.

smoothies for any reason

ENERGY BOOSTERS

HEALTH HELPERS

SANITY SAVERS

SPECIAL OCCASION SMOOTHIES

energy boosters...

The Pedigree of Honey
Does not concern the Bee—
A Clover, any time, to him,
Is Aristocracy.

EMILY DICKINSON

MELON JUICER

Reach for this hydrating blend after a hard workout.

1 cup lemon-lime sports drink
1 cup frozen honeydew chunks
1 cup watermelon chunks
1/2 cup lime sorbet
3 ice cubes, crushed

Pour sports drink into blender and add honeydew, watermelon, sorbet, and crushed ice. Blend at high speed until smooth.

BANANA-BERRY BREW

Spike your energy with this protein-rich fruity Smoothie.

1 cup chilled orange juice
1/2 cup non-fat blueberry yogurt
1 frozen banana
1 cup frozen strawberries
1 tablespoon brewer's yeast

Pour orange juice into blender and add yogurt, banana, strawberries, and brewer's yeast. Blend at high speed until smooth.

MIGHTY CARROT

Enjoy the earthy sweetness of
carrot-apple tinged with lemon,
and benefit from this protein
and antioxidant-rich blend!

1 cup chilled apple juice
1/4 cup shredded beet
1/2 cup frozen low-fat lemon yogurt
6 crushed frozen carrot juice cubes
1/2 cup crushed ice

Pour apple juice into blender and add beet,
yogurt, and crushed carrot juice cubes. Pulse
until combined, then add crushed ice and
blend at high speed until smooth.

BLACK-RASPBERRY REFUELER

Re-charge your battery with this vibrant blend of protein-rich yogurt and sweet, fiber-rich berries.

1 cup chilled cran-raspberry juice drink
1/2 cup non-fat vanilla yogurt
1 cup frozen blackberries
1/2 cup frozen raspberries
1/2 frozen banana

Pour cran-raspberry juice drink into blender and add yogurt, blackberries, raspberries, and banana. Blend at high speed until smooth.

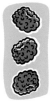

MANGO-A-GO-GO

Tea and mango go hand in hand in this Smoothie to get your heart pumping and keep it that way—safely. A great flavor combination that is sure to please.

1 cup chilled orange juice
1 cup frozen mango chunks
1/2 cup mango sorbet
6 crushed frozen black tea cubes

Pour orange juice into blender and add mango, sorbet, and crushed frozen tea cubes. Blend at high speed until smooth.

POTENT PEACH

The sweetness of peaches and honey—made extra special with fresh ginger and protein-rich tofu.

1 tablespoon fresh lemon juice
1 cup chilled peach nectar
1/4 cup soft silken tofu
1 tablespoon fresh grated ginger
2 tablespoons honey
1-1/2 cups frozen peach chunks

Pour lemon juice and peach nectar into blender and add tofu, ginger, honey, and peaches. Blend at high speed until smooth.

MOCHA ALMOND MAGIC

Without a doubt, the chocolate-coffee-almond flavors of this magical Smoothie will satisfy most every need and keep you coming back for more.

1/4 cup chilled strong black coffee
1 cup chilled almond milk
1-1/2 frozen bananas
1/4 cup sliced almonds
1/2 cup frozen non-fat chocolate yogurt

Pour coffee and almond milk into blender and add bananas, almonds, and yogurt. Blend at high speed until smooth.

PEANUT BUTTER BLAST

Count down and blast off with this decadent-tasting peanut-banana treat!

1 cup chilled non-fat milk
1-1/2 frozen bananas
1/2 cup frozen non-fat vanilla yogurt
2 tablespoons peanut butter
1/4 cup salted peanuts
1 tablespoon honey

Pour milk into blender and add bananas, yogurt, peanut butter, peanuts, and honey. Blend at high speed until smooth.

health
helpers...

An apple is an excellent thing—
until you have tried a peach.

GEORGE DU MAURIER

CRANBERRY COMFORTER

This pleasantly tart gingery blend soothes while it smooths, balancing sour cranberry and lemon with sweet raspberry-apple.

1 cup chilled cranberry juice cocktail
1 tablespoon fresh lemon juice
1/2 cup canned cranberry sauce
2 tablespoons applesauce
1 teaspoon fresh grated ginger
1/2 cup frozen raspberries
3 ice cubes, crushed

Pour cranberry juice cocktail and lemon juice into blender and add cranberry sauce, applesauce, ginger, raspberries, and crushed ice. Blend at high speed until smooth.

BETA BULLET

Loaded with flavor as well as in antioxidant-rich fruit!

1 cup chilled carrot juice
1 cup cantaloupe chunks
1/2 cup frozen peach chunks
1/2 cup frozen mango chunks

Pour carrot juice into blender and add cantaloupe, peaches, and mango. Blend at high speed until smooth.

FOUNTAIN OF YOUTH

Rewind the hands of time with this healthful wellspring of nutritious fresh fruits.

1 cup chilled apricot nectar
2 tablespoons fresh lemon juice
1/2 cup canned or fresh pineapple
1 cup frozen pitted cherries
1/2 cup frozen red grapes
3 ice cubes, crushed

Pour apricot nectar and lemon juice into blender and add pineapple, cherries, grapes, and crushed ice. Blend at high speed until smooth.

SKIN ILLUMINATOR

You'll feel like you're glowing after a few sips of this pale green pleaser!

1/2 cup chilled pineapple juice
1 cup seeded cucumber chunks
1/2 cup honeydew chunks
1/2 cup green apple chunks
2 tablespoons frozen apple juice concentrate
6 ice cubes, crushed

Pour pineapple juice into blender and add cucumber, honeydew, green apple, apple juice concentrate, and crushed ice. Blend at high speed until smooth.

COLD CHASER

Keep colds away with the disease-fighting antioxidants in this vitamin-rich Smoothie!

1 cup grapefruit juice
1 tablespoon fresh lemon juice
1 cup orange segments
1/2 cup pineapple chunks
1/2 cup strawberry sorbet
3 ice cubes, crushed

Pour grapefruit juice and lemon juice into blender and add oranges, pineapple, sorbet, and crushed ice. Blend at high speed until smooth.

HEART SAVER

With a blend like this, your heart can't help but say, "I love you, too."

1 cup chilled orange juice
1/2 cup cantaloupe chunks
5 dried apricots
1/2 cup strawberry sorbet
1 cup frozen seedless red grapes
3 ice cubes, crushed

Pour orange juice into blender and add cantaloupe, apricots, sorbet, grapes, and crushed ice. Blend at high speed until smooth.

GARDEN DEFENSE

Loaded with disease-fighting antioxidants to keep your immune system healthy and strong, this Smoothie can be like your personal bodyguard—ready to fight when the need arises.

1 cup chilled carrot juice
1 cup canned tomatoes with juice
1/2 cup red bell pepper chunks
1/2 cup avocado
2 tablespoons frozen orange juice concentrate
1 tablespoon (approximately) fresh parsley
3 ice cubes, crushed

Pour carrot juice into blender and add tomatoes, red bell pepper, avocado, orange juice concentrate, and parsley. Pulse until combined; then add crushed ice and blend at high speed until smooth.

LUCKY HEALTH CHARM

A healthful Smoothie charmed with the winning flavor combination of apples, carrots, and ginger.

1/2 cup chilled orange juice
1 cup carrot juice
2 tablespoons frozen apple juice concentrate
1 teaspoon fresh grated ginger
1/2 cup frozen green apple chunks
6 crushed frozen strong green tea cubes

Pour orange juice and carrot juice into blender and add apple juice concentrate, ginger, apples, and crushed tea cubes. Blend at high speed until smooth.

sanity
savers...

Once in a while I say, "Go for it"
and I eat chocolate.

CLAUDIA SCHIFFER

CHOCOLATE ESCAPE

You'll breathe a satisfied sigh of relief after one taste of this rich chocolate Smoothie.

1 cup chilled non-fat chocolate milk
1-1/2 frozen bananas
1/2 cup frozen non-fat chocolate yogurt
1/4 cup cashews

Pour chocolate milk into blender and add bananas, yogurt, and cashews. Blend at high speed until smooth.

CHEERY CHERRY

Find your smile with this cheery cherry-peach Smoothie!

1 cup chilled peach nectar
1/2 cup frozen low-fat peach yogurt
1 cup frozen pitted cherries
1/2 frozen banana

Pour peach nectar into blender and add yogurt, cherries, and banana. Blend at high speed until smooth.

SUBLIME KEY LIME

You'll feel sublime after tasting this
lime creamsicle Smoothie!

1/2 cup chilled non-fat milk
1 frozen banana
3/4 cup frozen non-fat vanilla yogurt
2 tablespoons honey
2 tablespoons fresh lime juice

Pour milk into blender and add banana,
yogurt, honey, and lime juice. Blend at high
speed until smooth.

STRESSLESS STRAWBERRY

Chill out with this creamy strawberry pleaser.

1 cup chilled vanilla soy milk
1/4 cup soft silken tofu
1 cup frozen strawberries
1/2 frozen banana
2 tablespoons frozen strawberry juice blend
    concentrate
1 teaspoon vanilla extract

Pour soy milk into blender and add tofu, strawberries, banana, strawberry juice blend concentrate, and vanilla extract. Blend at high speed until smooth.

OFF-DUTY ORANGE

This fruity orange Smoothie deserves your full attention, so sit back, put your feet up, and relax.

1 cup chilled orange juice
1/2 cup frozen strawberries
1/2 cup papaya chunks
1/2 frozen banana
3/4 cup orange sherbet

Pour orange juice into blender and add strawberries, papaya, banana, and sherbet. Blend at high speed until smooth.

PEACHY REVERIE

One taste of this peachy Smoothie and you'll know that dreams do come true after all.

1 cup chilled apple juice
1 cup frozen peach chunks
1/2 cup frozen blackberries
1/2 banana
1/2 cup peach sorbet

Pour apple juice into blender and add peaches, blackberries, banana, and sorbet. Blend at high speed until smooth.

RASPBERRY REDEMPTION

For sinners only.

1 cup non-fat milk
1-1/2 cups frozen raspberries
1/2 cup frozen non-fat vanilla yogurt
2 tablespoons frozen raspberry juice blend
  concentrate

Pour milk into blender and add raspberries, yogurt, and raspberry juice blend concentrate. Blend at high speed until smooth.

PEANUT BUTTER FUDGESICLE

You know you've just gotta try this peanutty fudge delight!

1 cup chilled non-fat chocolate milk
1 frozen chocolate Fudgesicle (stick removed!)
1-1/2 frozen bananas
2 tablespoons peanut butter

Pour chocolate milk into blender and add Fudgesicle, bananas, and peanut butter. Blend at high speed until smooth.

special
occasion
smoothies...

Florida oranges are so juicy that you
have to eat them in the bathtub.

CALIFORNIAN SAYING

BIRTHDAY BUBBLER

Cures whatever "ales" you!

1/2 cup chilled orange juice
1-1/2 cups frozen peach chunks
1/2 cup frozen strawberries
1 cup ginger ale

Pour orange juice into blender and add peaches and strawberries. Pulse until combined, then add ginger ale and blend at high speed until smooth.

New Year's Cheers

Add bubbly to this strawberry Smoothie for an extra fizzy New Year!

1 cup seltzer, divided
1-1/2 cups frozen strawberries
1/2 cup strawberry sherbet

Pour 1/2 cup seltzer into blender and add strawberries and sherbet. Pulse until combined; add remaining seltzer and blend at high speed until smooth.

GRADUATION CAPPER

After tossing your hat, it's time to celebrate with this delicious party pleaser. Here's to you!

2 tablespoons fresh lemon juice
1 cup lemon-lime soda, divided
1-1/2 cups frozen strawberries
1/2 cup orange sherbet

Pour lemon juice and 1/2 cup soda into blender and add strawberries and sherbet. Pulse until combined, then add remaining soda and blend at high speed until smooth.

HONEYMOON HARMONIZER

If oysters are the food of love, then cranberry juice is the beverage. Make every day magical with this healthful blend, and make your Honeymoon Harmonizer the start of living happily ever after!

1 cup red grapes
2 tablespoons fresh lemon juice
2 tablespoons grape juice concentrate
6 crushed frozen cranberry juice cubes

Add grapes, lemon juice, and grape juice concentrate to blender and pulse until combined. Add crushed cranberry juice cubes and blend at high speed until smooth. Add more juice to this tart blend if you prefer a thinner consistency.

PROMOTION COMMOTION

You did it! You're the greatest! Now celebrate with this fruity bubbler!

1-1/2 cups raspberry ginger ale, divided
1-1/2 cups canned or fresh pineapple
1/2 cup frozen raspberries

Pour 1 cup raspberry ginger ale into blender and add pineapple and raspberries. Pulse until combined, then add remaining soda and blend at high speed until smooth.

HOT DATE DELIGHT

Set the mood with this delicious cherry Smoothie. Garnish with a maraschino cherry to really impress your date.

1/2 cup chilled apple juice
1-1/2 cups frozen, pitted cherries
1/2 cup cherry ginger ale

Pour apple juice into blender and add cherries. Pulse until combined, then add ginger ale and blend at high speed until smooth

PARTY SIZZLER

What party wouldn't sizzle with a Smoothie like this? You've got passion, bubbles, and an element of surprise (the unexpected zing of ginger!).

1 cup chilled passion fruit juice
1 cup crushed pineapple
1/2 cup lemon sorbet
2 teaspoons fresh grated ginger
1/2 cup crushed ice
1/2 cup raspberry ginger ale
Fresh pineapple for garnish

Pour passion fruit juice into blender and add pineapple, sorbet, ginger, and crushed ice. Blend at high speed until smooth; add raspberry ginger ale and blend until combined. Garnish with fresh pineapple and a festive umbrella.

HOME ALONE CHILL OUT

You'll be dancing the fandango
after one sip of this creamy mango
Smoothie. Go ahead, no one's
looking.

1 cup chilled mango juice
1 cup frozen mango chunks
1/2 cup frozen, non-fat vanilla yogurt

Pour mango juice into blender and add
mango chunks and yogurt. Blend at high
speed until smooth.

INDEX OF SMOOTHIES BY PRIMARY INGREDIENT

APPLE

Early Apple 52
Icy Spicy Cider 109
Touchdown Apple 104

APRICOT

Apricot Awakening 88

BANANA

Almond Moon 79
Banana Blizzard 114
Banana-Berry Brew 124
Bedtime Banana 80
Call for Chocolate 73
Chai Time 65
Chocolate Escape 141
Delicious Daybreak 51
Espresso Boost 68
Java Jolt 69
Mocha Almond Magic . . 129
Nutty Nooner 60
Peanut Butter Blast 130
Peanut Butter Fudgesicle . 148

BLACKBERRY

Berry Break 67
Blackberry Bike Ride 98
Black-Raspberry Refueler . 126

BLUEBERRY

Blueberry Beginnings 50
Blueberry Bouquet 87
Rainy Day Blues 92

CANTALOUPE

Beta Bullet 133
Cantaloupe Croquet 94
Midday Melon 56

CARROT

Lucky Health Charm . . . 139
Mighty Carrot 125
Skinny Carrot Dipper . . . 99

CHERRY

Cheery Cherry 142
Cherry in a Hurry 62
Cherry Valentine 120
Fountain of Youth 134
Hot Date Delight 155

CRANBERRY

Cran-Apple Cool Down . 77
Cranberry Chiller 103
Cranberry Comforter . . . 132
Honeymoon
Harmonizer 153

CUCUMBER
Skin Illuminator 135

DATE
Homecoming Date 105

FIG
Fireside Figgy 108

GRAPE
Grand Slam Grape 91
Grape on the Go 59
Heart Saver 137

GRAPEFRUIT
Grapefruit Hail 113

GUAVA
Good Morning Guava ... 54

HONEYDEW
Home Run Honeydew .. 89
Melon Juicer 123

KIWIFRUIT
Extreme Skiwi 116
Kiwi Cocktail 74

LEMON
Citrus Crocus 85
Graduation Capper 152
Lemon Lift 71
Tee Time Lemon 90

LIME
Lunch Lime 58
Ski Lodge Lime 118
Sublime Key Lime 143

MANGO
Game, Set, Mango 100
Home Alone Chill Out . 157
Mango-a-Go-Go 127
Morning Mango 48

ORANGE
Cold Chaser 136
Holiday Orange 115
Off-Duty Orange 145
Orange Sunset 76
Sunshiny Citrus 53
Tangerine Warmer 117

PAPAYA
Perk-Me-Up Papaya 66

PASSION FRUIT
After Hours Passion 75

PEACH
Birthday Bubbler 150
Peachy Eats 57
Peachy Picnic 95
Peachy Reverie 146
Potent Peach 128

PEAR

Arm Chair Pear 82
Harvest Mixer 106
Pear-Apple Crisper 107

PINEAPPLE

Party Sizzler 156
Pineapple-Citrus Slush . . 112
Promotion Commotion . 154
Tropical Getaway 119

PLUM

Plum-Cherry Cooler 97

PUMPKIN

Pumpkin Pie Pleaser . . . 110

RASPBERRY

Raspberry Redemption . 147
Raspberry Refresher 70

Relaxing Raspberry 96
Rise 'n Raspberry 47
Sweet Berry Dreams 81

STRAWBERRY

New Year's Cheers 151
Oat to Lunch 61
Starry, Starry Strawberry . 78
Strawberry Patch Splendor . 86
Strawberry Sunrise 49
Stressless Strawberry . . . 144

TOMATO

Garden Defense 138
Tomatoes at Twelve 63

WATERMELON

Watermelon Splash 101